Relax,

It's Good For You

A Practical Guide for an Uptight World

Relax,

It's Good For You

A Practical Guide for an Uptight World

by Ed Bernd Jr.

First published in 1977

Revised and updated by the author

CreateSpace edition © Copyright 2014 by Ed Bernd Jr.

ISBN-13: 978-1496025722

ISBN-10: 1496025725

More titles by Ed Bernd Jr. available at

www.SilvaCourses.com

RELAX,
It's Good For You

Don't let stress become distress and ruin your life. Tension can hurt your health, hamper your relationships, curtail your ability to concentrate and learn, lower your productivity and creativity and problem solving ability, and undermine your self-confidence and happiness.

"Relax is a simple word, composed of only five letters. Assembling them into something more than a fond but unrealized ideal, however, is a task some of us find to be insurmountable. For me, the task has become far easier. I hope that you, too, can discover the real meaning of those five simple but important letters: RELAX."

- From the Foreword by Hubert Griggs

Ed Bernd Jr. first started teaching the Silva Mind Control Method in 1977, and continues to promote and teach Jose Silva's last course, the Silva UltraMind ESP System.

Jose Silva with Ed Bernd Jr.

Ed is no stranger to stress, mental or physical: An award winning police reporter on metropolitan daily newspapers for ten years, he has lived with stress in all its forms; as a polio survivor at age five, who learned to walk again, he knows about physical stress, too.

Foreword

by Hubert Griggs

When I first learned that Ed Bernd Jr. was conducting seminars in "relaxation" my first reaction was, "Who needs it?"

Then I had second thoughts.

"If I'm so good at relaxing" I wondered, "why is the doctor telling me I have a pre-ulcer condition?"

The seed had taken root, and when Ed told me I could learn to relax in the midst of stress, as well as on weekends, and that the techniques he teaches would help me approach the inevitable tasks that I did not relish with a more positive attitude -possibly even one of enjoyment - it blossomed.

Since that time, I have participated in The Relaxation Seminar. I would not presume to promise to anyone else the benefits I believe I have received, because I cannot guarantee anyone else's state of mind.

I do, however, believe that anyone who is willing to listen with a reasonably open mind, anyone who is willing to apply some simple techniques, even half as often as recommended, can derive some real benefits.

Relax is a simple word, composed of only five letters. Assembling them into something more than a fond but unrealized ideal, however, is a task some of us find to be insurmountable. For me, the task has become far easier. I hope that you, too, can discover the real meaning of those five simple but important letters: RELAX.

-Hubert Griggs has been in the newspaper business since 1960, serving as an editor on two daily newspapers in the Cocoa Beach, Fla., area. He also served as chief investigator in the county solicitors' office (the county's chief criminal prosecutor).

Introduction

Are you in control of your life? Can you say: "I am the master of my fate, the captain of my soul"?

Or do you feel like so many people in our urbanized, mechanized, computerized world: frustrated victims of the times, who react to circumstances that come upon them rather than being able to take full control of life.

To bring your life - your emotions, your mind - under control, there is no better place to begin than with stress. Or more correctly, distress.

If you can learn to handle tension and distress within yourself, then you have taken the first basic step towards taking full control of what happens in your life.

You can learn to control your habits, your weight, your health, the time you get up in the morning and how you feel when you get up, headaches, sleep, dreams, concentration and retention of information (memory), creativity, your relationships with other people. You can learn to develop your intuition and use it accurately and reliably to make the right decisions and to correct problems.

How many of the problems that confront people are caused by tension, stress, frustration, worry, and wrong decisions?

Mark Twain said, "Temper is what gets most of us into trouble. Pride is what keeps us there."

If we can learn to control our own emotions and reactions, to control whether we become tense and upset or take things in stride, that's a big step. Then we can learn to control other facets of our lives.

Of course, for those who live in a constant state of tension and distress, learning to control this could be a sufficient goal in itself.

But there's so much more, once you start to achieve more control of your life.

If a student has greater control, he can make better grades.

As a housewife develops more control, she has a happier family.

When a businessman takes greater control of his life, he will have more business.

Everyone can make better decisions when they are relaxed. You can think more clearly, process information better, and your intuition works best when you are relaxed.

How do we begin gaining control, how do we learn to subdue tensions?

Let's began with an in-depth examination of stress, tension and distress.

Chapter 1

A chief of high rank and great holiness in New Zealand happened to leave the remains of his meal by the roadside. A young slave came along, a strong healthy fellow, who saw what was left over and started to eat it. Hardly had he finished when a horrified spectator informed him of his offense in eating the meal of the chief. The man had been a strong brave warrior, but as soon as he heard this he collapsed and was afflicted by terrible convulsions, from which he died toward sunset of the following day.

-Sigmund Freud, Totem and Taboo

What could have caused such a sudden and mysterious demise in a young, strong warrior? Maybe a psychologically stressful situation, bringing about muscle electrical instability and ventricular fibrillation in his heart?

In other words, was he scared to death?

If a stressful situation could produce such results in one so young, brave and strong, one in peak physical health, then what can stress do to those of us who get little physical exercise, who have little outlet for bottled up emotions and frustrations?

How many of the 400,000 Americans who die suddenly each year from coronary heart disease are the victims of stress?

Stress is a part of life. And it is something that is important to our survival, growth and progress. But when we let stress become distress, when we let it affect our lives, our health and happiness, then something's got to be done.

Stress - or more correctly our inability to cope with stress, or distress - adversely affects our physical health, mental health, peace of mind, interpersonal relationships, causes us to lose sleep, affects our appetites, even our sex life, causes headaches, migraines, ulcers, heart disease, constipation, can keep us from advancing in our careers, limits our productivity and creativity, fosters bad habits and undermines our self confidence.

Dr. Hans Selye, a world authority on stress, has called it the number one health problem in the world today, and adds that medical research has demonstrated that stress causes ulcers, heart attacks, hypertension, migraine headaches, mental illness, and even certain types of arthritis.

Stress is responsible for aging, and it also contributes to cancer, according to Dr. Selye, who has written more than 30 books on the subject.

Besides leading to diseases that could drastically shorten a person's life, stress also lowers resistance to diseases such as pneumonia, according to medical people. And people under stress are more likely to become involved in accidents - in their car, on the job, in the home.

A strong indictment of a phenomenon that has been a fact of life as long as humans have inhabited Planet Earth?

Yes, but true. And logical..

A whole big list of diseases has become popular in the "Industrial Age." Like hypertension.

The cause-effect relationship of stress and hypertension (which leads to high blood pressure which in turn is associated with heart attacks) is clearly demonstrated by Dr. Herbert Benson in his book, *The Relaxation Response*.

How often does stress interfere with our meals, upsetting our digestion, or even turning us away from the table at minor annoyances like a child spilling catsup on your new slacks or dress? And how much does this lack of proper nourishment in turn affect our health?

Our industrialized, urbanized Western society has become one that functions on millions of tranquilizers per year. Not to mention oceans of alcohol needed for "relaxation" and the newest "goodies" - drugs like marijuana which are often used as an escape from a stress-filled environment. Some people don't bother with all that: they just drift into a fantasy world called "Mental Illness."

How many fathers come home, tired from a day of stress at the office, in the world of commerce or business, and just shout at the wife and kids to "Be quiet and let me relax!"

For many people, the only way to get to a full night's sleep is with the aid of pills, barbiturates which interfere with the normal, necessary sleep cycles and leave a person still tired in the morning, needing amphetamines to "get going" again. The alcohol-coffee connection has the same detrimental effect.

Scores of headache remedies are advertised to help us get rid of tension-induced headaches, headaches we could rid ourselves of within a couple of minutes - if we but knew how to relax.

How often do we develop "mental blocks" when put under pressure? How much does this hamper our creativity, our productivity, the things we need to advance ourselves in our jobs, our careers?

How many of our habits - cigarette smoking, drinking, even sex - are simply things we use to burn off the immediate torture of the stress we have built up and know not how to cope with?

And how much does this stress, which comes with one or more of the above problems, undermine our self-confidence, our self-image, our belief in our ability to live a good life, meeting life's obstacles successfully?

The case against stress is strong. There are many books detailing many research reports if you want to read them (there is a list at the back of this book).

But the real question is: "What can we do about stress?"

First, let's find out what causes stress.

Chapter 2

A young newspaper reporter was sent to interview an Indian Chief on the Chief's 150th birthday. "To what do you attribute your great age, Chief?" the reporter asked. "Me never argue," the Chief answered. "That's wonderful," the reporter said, "but surely there must be more to it than that!" "Hmm," the Chief paused. "You may be right."

If we could all learn to take things as easily as the old Chief, we'd have few stress-related problems in our lives.

But we are not built that way.

Why?

It goes way back.

As our cave man ancestors walked through the jungles, searching for food, they were followed by various beasts who considered the cave man a very tasty morsel.

When a tiger would leap, so would the cave man.

Why?

Because he had a gland in the brain, the pituitary gland, that regulates the endocrine system, which would cause the adrenal glands to secrete a tiny amount of the hormone adrenaline to produce a sudden burst of energy for running away if possible, or fighting if necessary.

While the adrenal gland was causing a sudden release of sugar into the blood, the brain was instructing the other organs to prepare for the strenuous effort to come: the heart would pump more rapidly, the lungs would begin to take in more oxygen and all systems would gear up to maximum.

Suddenly, the cave man had a lot of extra energy for a short period of time. He was capable of fighting off, or running away from, that tiger with some degree of success.

The people who were best at this were the people who survived. So naturally, the way evolution goes, we still have that particular system - like it or not.

But in our society, there are no more tigers. Yet we have a very well developed mechanism for fending off threats to our lives.

Or... things that we perceive to be threats to our very root security. Or for that matter, threats to even small portions of our environment, little pieces of our security.

If someone threatens to fire us, who has the ability to fire us, thereby cutting off our means of supporting ourselves and our families, we trigger the flight or fight mechanism.

Even a mild rebuke, perhaps just a frown in our direction, can trigger this reaction in us. Why?

Because even more important than our economic security, very often, if the integrity of our images of ourselves. Something that embarrasses us, holds us up to ridicule, makes us feel we cannot cope with things - this seems to trigger a more severe response even than a threat of monetary loss.

Most of us could better cope with monetary loss to a robber than we can tolerate an insult from a loved one.

This is easy to understand:

The social instinct that drives us to seek the approval and support of other members of our own species is a fundamental program to help insure the survival of the species as well as the survival of individuals of that species.

And there are so many threats to our self-image, to our belief in our own importance:

*The driver who pulls out in front of us and triggers this primitive reaction.

*The noises of our industrialized urbanized world that assault us with unnatural sounds; uncomfortable furniture and clothing; temperatures we don't like.

*The constant assault from media advertising, junk mail and telephone solicitors who come right into our homes uninvited via Mr. Bell's invention.

*Even television programs clamoring for attention and "Neilsen ratings."

Even the feeling that you are going to "miss out on something" adds to stress. It could keep you from having a relaxing vacation if you see your two weeks of "freedom" - freedom from stress - washing away in daily rains.

Change usually causes stress - change for good as well as bad. A new job, a move to another city, gaining or losing a spouse, changes in recreational activity, even Christmas can cause stress.

We are a nation of affluence - even those barely getting by are better off than the richest people of just a century ago, before the advent of electrical appliances and paved streets and cars and airplanes and television and TV dinners and indoor plumbing. If you think it's not stressful walking through snow on a winter morning just to get to the bathroom, then try it!

Yet in spite of all this affluence - or perhaps because of it - very often we still are not happy:

If we have something, we are willing to fight to keep it.

If we don't have something, and we feel we can't get it, we have to adjust our self-image - our concepts of our true value - to cope with those facts.

No matter what, it seems we are destined to frustration. To stress.

For the cave man, this was no particular problem. His system triggered the flight-or-fight reaction, and he fled or fought. He had something definite and immediate to do to burn up the energy.

He would run away from the danger, or if necessary he would fight it.

But today, we don't turn and run away, and we don't get into fights. Not in the physical sense, at least. We do have all this extra energy coming to us. And we do nothing to dissipate it. To burn it up.

So we are left with our whole system geared up, our heart beating faster, our blood pressure up, our muscles tensed, everything on alert and ready. And that leaves us with:

Hypertension.

Which is associated with those illnesses of the industrial age, the illnesses you won't find in remote, primitive tribal villages.

Most of us are not even aware of the magnitude of the stress that we carry around with us in our daily lives. It is only when we learn to relax and let go that we begin to learn how much stress we have within us.

Many psychologists and psychiatrists will give you reasons for stress in your life. They will talk about everything that happened to you from birth on, and sometimes even prior to birth. The way you were toilet trained, they will tell you, affects you today and can cause or prevent distress in your life.

Deadlines, too many problems, wrong decisions and indecision, and the feeling of having done "too little too late" all bring on distress.

But what it all boils down to is attitude.

A thing can cause you distress only if it is a threat to you in some fashion, and it is a threat only if, for some reason, you perceive it as a threat.

If you are insulted by a person whose opinion means nothing to you, you will not become distressed. In fact, it might please you. But a frown from a loved one can make you feel sick inside.

A threat from an inept subordinate that "I'll have your job someday!" may make you laugh, while the same threat from a member of the board of directors could send you straight to a session with your favorite bartender.

Your reaction depends on your attitude. And your attitude has been shaped into what it is today by a lot of things that happened to you in the past. Things that we can not go back and change, cannot erase.

While we cannot change the things that shaped our attitudes, we can neutralize them by restructuring our attitudes once we have an understanding of what needs changing and we find an effective way to do this.

So the first step is to learn to relax. For when we are excited, when our system is all geared up for flight-or-fight, then our thinking is distorted by the immediate situation, the urgent threat that must be dealt with and eliminated, and creative, long range planning to effectively deal with the situation is not even considered.

Actually, we can use this built-up emotional energy to reprogram, to restructure our attitudes, but only when we understand that we can do this, and also know how to go about doing this. And even while we have all this built up emotion, we must have a certain calm within us, a certain understanding, to begin to cope effectively.

Scientists recently have found that a chemical substance in the brain, norepinephrine, is important in attention, sleep and learning. Norepinephrine is the opposite of adrenaline, so when we trigger the flight or fight response and its adrenaline, we will find it very difficult to use our full mental capacities to think logically and creatively, and to absorb information for future use. In many ways, the flight or fight response channels our energies into physical outlets at the expense of mental acuity and the ability to let the body rest and recuperate.

Dr. Selye says one of the most prevalent causes of stress - or distress - in our modern world is, the lack of goals, the absence of motivation. In recent years, religious values have seemed irrelevant to many people; money is not a major goal of many young people; there is little allegiance to national leaders. All this leaves people with lots of energy but nothing to use it on. It is important to have a purpose.

Dr. Selye quotes his favorite French author, Montaigne, who said, "No wind blows in favor of the ship that has no port of destination."

So how can we cope with stress? Let's look at what the experts suggest.

Chapter 3

As a truck driver sat in a roadside diner preparing to eat the steak dinner he had just been served, three members of a motorcycle gang came in and sat on both sides of him. Without saying anything, they took the trucker's dinner and began eating it themselves.

Without a word, the truck driver got up, paid the bill and left.

"He sure wasn't much of a man, was he?" one cyclist said to the waitress.

"No, and he isn't much of a truck driver either," she answered. "He ran over three motorcycles trying to get out of the parking lot!"

If we could all get rid of our tensions and frustrations by taking direct physical action, we would have much less problem with stress than we have today. But most of us can't do that. It just isn't practical.

So instead we must look for ways to neutralize the energy we build up from these stress-producing situations.

The things we do to dissipate the energy seem to have a lot to do with the quality of our lives.

* If we suppress the energy, keep it bottled up, then distress can manifest as dis-ease, like hypertension, heart disease and ulcers, among others.

* If we direct our energy towards ourselves, it can manifest as alcoholism, drug addiction, or suicide.

* If we direct it towards others, it can come out as criminal activity, or, on a lesser scale, very poor relationships with other people.

So how do we learn to relax?

Relax.

It's an easy word to say. It slides right through the mouth and rolls off the tongue.

But it's not so easy to do.

The flight or fight response, which has been with us for a couple of million years, has become completely automatic, an unconscious reaction most of us trigger many times a day.

Relaxation - real, effective, beneficial relaxation we can use to improve our health and our productivity and our lives - is something we have to consciously do.

If you are in good physical condition, then hard physical work or exercise can help, but throwing golf clubs in disgust, cursing tangled fishing line, berating your tennis partner... these are not effective means of relaxation. Recreation, perhaps. But not effective relaxation.

The effective relaxation comes when all our bodily systems slow down, when we take a little time to "shut out the static in our heads," to reflect upon ourselves and our futures.

Scientists have found that we are effectively relaxing when our heartbeat slows, our respiration and oxygen consumption rate decreases, and the electrical energy that powers our computer-like brain slows to the "alpha rhythm."

We might be able to relax a little with drugs or alcohol, but that is not very beneficial. In fact, it is often quite harmful. The consumption of drugs changes body-brain chemistry, dulls the edge of creativity and inventiveness, weakens decision making abilities and intuition.

And when we "relax" this way, we have less control, when what we want is more control.

We can relax with the right kind of music, with creative daydreaming, even with sleep - if we can relax long enough to go to sleep when we need to relax.

But our Puritan work ethic seems to interfere if we simply try to take an hour off to listen to beautiful music, or to just sit and daydream.

So what is the solution?

We can find a teacher or a book to give us a specific method which we can follow, a habit forming practice that will evoke relaxation when we need it.

Can you do it on your own, without having a teacher?

Yes. But it will be difficult; it will take a lot of determination, and a lot of faith that you are doing the right thing, because it will take you quite a while to verify it. But it has been done by a few. You have to do it without "trying." After all, you cannot force yourself to relax!

Until you acquire a method and become proficient at it, what can you do?

Some of the answers are short range and can help with the immediate problem, while others are of a more long range variety.

*When you feel stress strike, just take a deep breath. Tell yourself that every time you take a deep breath, you will relax. Physical and mental relaxation will tend to go together, and your breath can serve as a link between your body and mind.

*For physical relaxation, instruct your muscles to relax. If you first tense a muscle, then relax it, you can really feel the effect. Start with the muscles around your eyes, your jaw, your neck and shoulders and work down to your toes.

*For mental relaxation, practice visualizing passive and tranquil scenes. Imagine yourself at a place where you can completely relax. The sport of golf probably offers more benefit in the form of relaxation than in physical exercise, and this seems to be because of the mental attitude that goes with it.

Being in open space, away from telephones, close to nature, seems to be very relaxing, so imagine yourself in a place like this.

*You have the ability to think about your thoughts. Humans may be the only animals who have the ability to be aware that they are aware. So step back, so to speak, and look at your reaction, your response, your attitude, your thoughts. Ask yourself exactly what it is you are reacting to. Why are you reacting? Does it have something to do with a conditioned response from your past? Is it really your problem, or is it a problem that belongs to the person who is posing a threat to you?

*Pretend it is happening to someone else. Look for the humor in the situation (there is seldom a situation without humor - if this is truly that serious a situation, like a life or death situation from an accident or something, then you probably need the energy you have built up from the stress and will dissipate it with natural means.)

*Ask yourself if this problem will seem important ten years from now. Or even one year from now. How many of the problems that seemed so serious ten years ago actually affect your life today?

*Remind yourself that "This, too, shall pass. Those four words can work magic, for nothing is permanent. Everything is temporary, except for our consciousness deep within.

*If you are religious, remember that God is with you always. He is for you, though He may sometimes let you encounter obstacles so you can grow stronger by handling them, coping with them. If God be for me, who can be against me? As a Nun once told me, "God doesn't make junk!"

*Remember that all humans make mistakes. It is part of life, just as problem solving is part of life. And we don't find the solution to a problem, we don't correct mistakes, by studying the problem. Instead we should look for the solution.

*Re-channel your energy into a constructive use, such as making a friend of your enemy.

*Motion has been found helpful in inducing relaxation. The movement of a boat, a swing, a rocking chair, or just "swaying" might help.

* It is only logical to believe that we are all on this earth for some reason, some purpose, and if we are fulfilling that purpose, we have nothing to worry about; our needs will be taken care of, one way or another. Not necessarily all of our desires, but all of our needs.

You can get rid of stress in your life by ridding yourself of guilt and irrational fear. If you have system of relaxation that uses the alpha rhythm then you can "reprogram" the guilts and fears while relaxing.

Guilts and fears make us feel insecure. They eat away at our ego, our self-image. If we don't have a good self-image, we don't feel secure. And if we don't feel secure, we won't relax.

If we won't relax, we are more susceptible to stress; we will trigger it more often, and perhaps more severely.

And, as we said before, this affects our health. Studies by Drs. Bernard Lown, Richard Verrier and Ramon Corbalan of the Harvard School of Public Health's Cardiovascular Laboratory, have produced some suggestions for relaxation to lower the risk of heart disease; in a recent study, they found that sleep was better than even the most powerful cardiac drugs in controlling dangerous heartbeats in some patients.

They go on to recommend moderate exercise and meditation for both physical and psychological benefits.

The best safeguard against the risk of sudden death, they say, is relaxation.

So how do we handle self-image problems, old guilts and irrational fears that produce stress?

Methods range from lengthy and expensive psychoanalysis, to some of the more radical methods of deliberately triggering trauma in order to immediately relive the "cause" of our "problems."

In between are other methods, such as looking within while relaxing at the alpha levels in the practice known as meditation. Some forms of meditation simply clear the mind of conscious thought, and health gradually improves and problems slowly fade away, often without any conscious effort on your part.

Some of the new methods of meditation developed in the West, sometimes termed "Dynamic Meditation," reap the benefits of traditional Eastern and early Christian meditation practices while at the same time using these levels in a scientific manner to solve problems simply, effectively, speedily, thus eliminating the cause of much stress. The book *Jose Silva's Everyday ESP* by Jose Silva Jr. tells how.

You can learn faster with the audio recordings of Jose Silva's UltraMind ESP System.

Even better is to attend a live Silva UltraMind presentation.

There are other things you can do to solve purely physical problems that lead to stress:

*Check your nutritional program, make sure you are getting a balanced diet every day, with adequate vitamins and minerals. The book, *Let's Eat Right to Keep Fit* by Adelle Davis, a bio-chemist and nutrition researcher, is a good place to begin.

*Make sure your mealtimes are pleasant times. Mealtimes should not be used as convenient gatherings of the clan to mete out retribution and punishment.

*Practice holding your head high when you walk. Like you're

trying to touch the ceiling with your head. Good posture helps alleviate stress.

*Sit in chairs that are really comfortable. Chairs that allow you to sit straight comfortably You need good support for your lower back; a small pillow in your lower back (especially when driving) often helps. It is better not to cross your legs, as this tilts the pelvis, which throws the spine out of line, which causes the head to tilt to compensate - all making you uncomfortable.

*Balance is important. Stand evenly on both feet. Don't let one hand do all the work - use both hands. Shift packages, brief cases or purses from one hand to the other so you don't tire out one side of your body. Remain refreshed overall.

*Sleep on a firm mattress. Sleeping on your stomach on a soft mattress causes your back to arch, causing discomfort, loss of beneficial sleep and stress.

*Watch less television. According to Dr. Clancy D. McKenzie, we often work out our aggressive fantasies during exciting television programs, and this is not relaxing. It can trigger a version of the flight-or-fight response.

*If noise is a problem where you live, ear plugs might be a viable solution. Other tips for noise include: use carpeting and draperies to deaden noise; select quiet-running appliances (have them demonstrated before buying); mount stationary appliances on sound deadening material, such as rubber mats; use other sound deadening material around appliances - fiberglass, etc. Also, associate noises with happy thoughts - change your attitude: let the noise of children bring to mind happy childhood memories from your past; think of the fun of flying in the blue when you hear jets overhead. Leave closet doors open at night to absorb noise. Use plastic lined, cloth shower curtains.

*In your home, colors, lighting, placement of furniture, even the kind of furniture can either add to a relaxing atmosphere or to stress. Use soft or indirect lighting for relaxation, use pastel colors such as light blues and greens; group furniture close, in a friendly "tribal circle"; use rooms only for what they are intended - banish the television from the bedroom and the dining room; give children their own "territory"; keep it simple, uncluttered, both in the amount of furniture and the kind of furniture - elaborate designs and patterns can sometimes be stressful.

*Dress comfortably, or as comfortably as you can for your job. And dress the way you feel you should - you get right back into self-image problems if you feel uncomfortable with the way you dress. Don't go without a bra just because other women do; if it makes you feel uncomfortable, this creates stress. Don't wear a leisure suit and get a mod haircut because that's what younger businessmen are doing; if you feel you look foolish, this undermines your self-image, your self-confidence, your ability to relax, your ability to be effective, creative and productive.

*Perhaps one of the best and most important things we could do to become more aware of our true potential, our real value, our perfectness, is simply to take time out to evaluate ourselves.

Dr. Maxwell Maltz in his book *Conquest of Frustration* says the first hour we are awake in the morning is the most important hour we have in the entire day, for it is during this hour we can set the tone for the entire day: if we begin the day by imagining ourselves doing well, getting along with everyone, being creative, then we have a much better chance of that happening.

And in the evening, before retiring, we can review the day and make sure we have learned from our mistakes and, most importantly, forgiven ourselves.

Many people report that the greatest value a consciousness-raising program - meditation, religion, or whatever - has for them is the realization, not intellectually but experientially, that they are something more than the finite physical body and the emotions and personality.

There is something deep within that transcends all this, that is lasting and permanent. There is something within you that is crying to be expressed.

But this is something you can't incorporate into your life by reading about it. You've got to experience it first hand.

Chapter 4

There is a Sufi story about an elderly king who offered to pass on his kingdom to whoever could catch and ride a wild stallion that roamed freely in the town.

One strong young man chased the horse relentlessly, with great will, but without success. Finally the young man's brother pointed out to him he would never catch the horse by chasing after him, and suggested that he chase the horse in a certain direction while the brother waited there and caught him.

They agreed and did so, and came riding up to the king on the stallion.

The king rewarded both of them equally with his kingdom, the one for his action, the other for his wisdom.

This is the age of the computer. How would you like to own your own biological electronic computer, a computer that would give you personalized readouts for programs to bring about complete physical relaxation at any time of the day or night?

A computer that could tell you exactly what you should eat and when to give you maximum nutrition and to maintain your ideal weight?

A computer that would take stock of your physical inventory and give you a tailor-made exercise program to get you into the exact physical condition you consider perfect for you?

A computer that can solve business problems for you, work out solutions that are perfect for you because they take into consideration your own skills, goals, talents, ability, motivation and drive?

You want a computer like that?

Okay, you've got it!

Where is it? you ask.

On top of your shoulders. Right inside your own head.

Your brain is a bio-computer, more complex, capable of handling more problems and functions than any computer that will ever be built.

It is there for you to use, to relax, to solve problems, to control habits, to control health, to file information for future use, to do virtually anything you consider important in your life.

Like any other computer, it can be programmed. It will work best when programmed in a certain way.

It seems to function most efficiently when the electrical energy that powers it pulsates at about ten cycles per second, at what is known as alpha frequency.

What is alpha?

Alpha brainwave activity is an indication that a person is using both brain hemispheres to think with. That is: the person is able to think (function) with the creative and intuitive right-brain hemisphere as well as the logical, rational and scientific left-brain hemisphere.

And, like our example in the Sufi story, when you function with both brain hemispheres, you can accomplish far more than you can when using one brain hemisphere only.

Scientists who have studied people who are very creative, and studied people like Swami Rama of India who can control many physical functions like heartbeat and blood pressure and pain, have found that these people usually have a very high alpha output.

It is these alpha brain waves that serve as the foundation of the interest in "biofeedback training" which uses sophisticated instrumentation to help people learn to get in touch with themselves.

By learning to reach alpha, patients using biofeedback equipment can induce relaxation and speed healing time as much as tenfold, it has been reported.

But alpha is not a panacea. It is no automatic cure for all our problems.

What it is, is another dimension of mind that we can use to help solve problems.

Previously, our culture has taught us only how to use the rational, scientific, analyzing, doubting, "beta" part of our minds.

Now we know that besides the faster beta brain wave frequencies, we have the slower alpha frequencies, the level where we go within and tap the genius that resides inside each of us.

Alpha brain waves are not new, of course, but were not discovered until the 1920's when electrical activity was first discovered in the human brain. Even though alpha brain wave frequencies were unknown, they have been used by yogis and hypnotists and Zen masters and writers and artists and businessmen for a long, long time.

The first electrical activity ever measured in the brain was at about ten cycles per second, just about in the middle of the normal range we use in a 24-hour period: .5 to 20 cycles per second.

This seems to be the most energetic frequency and therefore the one first detected.

Since these are the strongest, most energetic frequencies, scientists surmise that this might be the "place" where the brain could function most effectively and efficiently.

Experience seems to prove this out:

*You can retain much more of a lecture if you listen at alpha.

*Healing is speeded up at alpha.

*It is easier to "reprogram" habits and attitudes at alpha.

*Solutions to problems seem to come faster at alpha.

And it seems that anyone spending very much time at alpha -
45 minutes a day for instance - just automatically gains more
self-confidence, a better self-image, a knowledge that the true
self is something more than the physical, "beta" world of things
and desires and personality.

But still, alpha is not a panacea.

For one thing, you have to discipline yourself to "go to
alpha" on a regular basis. Without training, most people simply
fall asleep when they go to alpha. That's the most natural thing
to do.

Once at alpha, you need to know what to do to reprogram,
to improve health, to solve problems, to eliminate habits.

These things are not difficult, but the computer - the brain -
takes instructions very literally and you have to be careful to
give it just the right instructions. You might get rid of one
problem at alpha, only to cause another one, because the
computer doesn't reason; it only carries out instructions.

Dr. Benson, in his book, *The Relaxation Response*, says there
are four basic elements necessary for meditation: a quiet
environment, an object to dwell upon, a passive attitude, and a
comfortable position.

Combine these four elements, dwell on one single thought
for a half hour and you'll probably be producing alpha waves.

Or you can pay a hypnotist to use his induction procedures
to take you to another state of mind where he can program you
with whatever you desire. It might be at alpha, or at theta,
which is about 5 cycles per second.

Or you can use one of the methods of "autogenic" training, where the biocomputer - the brain - is programmed to produce alpha on demand.

With autogenic training (as little as three hours is all it takes) you can produce alpha on demand by going through a simple procedure. At the office, in a restaurant, at home, watching a parade. The amount of alpha produced will be influenced by environmental conditions, but you can learn to increase alpha on demand.

Whatever method you use, it is certainly worth the effort and the cost, even if just for the relaxation benefits alone.

Then you add the other benefits, there is no way to place a value on it.

Previously, as the famous professor William James of Harvard said many years ago, "Compared to what we ought to be, we are only half awake. We are making use of only a small part of our physical and mental resources. Stating the thing broadly, the human individual thus lives far within his limits. He possesses powers of various sorts which he habitually fails to use."

Alpha brain waves, the "inner conscious levels," had not even been discovered back then, but how right the great psychologist was.

Better health - productivity - creativity - happiness - habit control - faster learning - self-confidence - problem-solving ability - better interpersonal relationships - better decision making - enhanced intuition - all these things are related to alpha.

Dr. O. Carl Simonton reports that he treats terminal cancer patients by having them spend 15 minutes at alpha three times a day. This has been extremely successful.

Thomas Edison, the creative genius who put more patents on

the books than any other inventor in the history of the United States, knew how to use the inner conscious levels and his right-brain hemisphere to solve problems - even though alpha brain waves had never been heard of:

Edison used to work hard in his research at beta, the faster brain wave frequencies. Then when he would reach a "sticking point," he would take one of his famous "cat naps." He would doze off in his favorite chair, holding steel balls in his hands.

As he would fall asleep - drifting into alpha - his arms would relax and lower, letting the balls fall into pans on the floor. The noise would wake Edison, and very often he would awaken with an idea to continue with his project.

What might this genius have done if he had known how to use alpha levels consciously, without falling asleep to get there?

After all, what is a genius? Aren't geniuses just people who uses more of their minds than the people who are not thought of as a geniuses?

Aren't geniuses people who think at an inner, intuitive level where they can grasp the answers to more questions than the average person?

Do you want to think and act like a genius?

Are you making conscious use of just half the ability you have? Would you be satisfied with this?

Perhaps you, like Edison, use this "alpha awareness" unconsciously, without knowing or planning.

How much more effective could you be if you used alpha levels consciously, creatively, constructively, and continuously?

Can you imagine if most people only used one of their two legs? If only a few people realized that they could use both legs, those 2-legged people would look "super human" to the rest who only used one leg.

The good news is: You have two brain hemispheres just like the geniuses do; and you can learn to function with conscious awareness in two dimensions just like the geniuses do:

You can learn to use the powerful, creative, intuitive alpha level to think with, and the active beta level to act on your decisions.

During the last several years, I've investigated everything from aerobics and acupuncture to yoga and Zen to learn how to manage and dissipate stress. Since I have chosen to live a high-stress lifestyle, I have experimented on myself.

Years ago, I used alcohol - I would drink to excess, so my body could dissipate excess stress overcoming hangovers. I've used exercise, writing, art, karate, weightlifting, running ... you name it, I've probably tried it.

The one thing that I found that worked for me and still works is the Jose Silva's mind training system. It works because it is not just an "aspirin." Instead, it is a comprehensive System that lets me channel the energies and emotions that I generate into creative solutions to the challenges I encounter in my life.

We all encounter challenges in life. That is what life is all about. That is the only way we can possibly learn, and we must learn in order to grow, and we must grow so we can accomplish more, can have more fun, can earn more.

But growth means change. And change means threat.

Let us review for a moment just how we function in the physical world:

We have biological programming for survival.

We have programming that we are born with to insure the survival of the individual, and the survival of the species.

For the individual to survive, we need food, water, air. We need the protection of the group.

For the species to survive, we need to reproduce our kind. And again, we see the social motive coming into play; we need other people both for protection, and for procreation.

Any change could be a threat to the survival of the individual or the species.

Thus, we have been programmed to view any change or anything new in the environment as a possible threat until we have found otherwise.

And we humans have been blessed with imagination, something that appears to be unique to our species. So very often, we let this imagination amplify the new situation, until it builds to incredible stress levels, thanks to the ancient flight or fight mechanism. For instance, we might worry for days about someone's opinion of us, because of some minor action or comment we made.

And many people try to meet the stresses that are generated by seeking those things necessary for survival: more food, something to drink, something to fill our lungs (cigarette smoke).

If our imagination has the ability to amplify potential stress situations, and the capacity to remind us of those situations long after they have passed, then is it also possible to learn to control the imagination in a way that helps us decrease stress without having to indulge in activities that are destructive to the body?

Of course it is.

That is where Jose Silva's UltraMind ESP System comes in.

I still find it useful to use exercise to drain off some of the energy I build up in my busy lifestyle. And I find meditation a very useful tool to help me achieve some very peaceful and beautiful moments during the day. And I eat a very nutritious diet, and avoid placing unnecessary environmental stresses on my body.

But the key to my success in staying calm and relaxed and healthy and happy and productive is my ability to use the tools I was born with to help me successfully meet every situation I encounter.

I do not dread facing the day when I wake up in the morning. And I do not worry about what happened during the day when I get into bed at night. Instead, I use the mental tools I possess - I use my imagination - to deal with situations, to plan, to make decisions, to understand.

As I mentioned before, it is easier to experience than to explain. The logical left-brain hemisphere cannot always understand an experience, but the right-brain hemisphere knows exactly what it means.

The mental energies always must be dealt with. It will not suffice to deal with only the physical manifestations, through chemistry for instance. Nor is it sufficient to escape into "spiritual enlightenment," or intoxication. We are here on his planet to do a job. We've been equipped to do it. We must stay and do it.

The tools are now here to enable us to do the job, to express all of our human potential and use our fantastic minds and imaginations to improve ourselves and also to improve conditions on this planet, instead of creating more problems. We owe thanks to Jose Silva for discovering the new science of psychorientology: the orienting or directing of the psyche, or mind. "Mind Control."

It is through taking more control of the tools we have to work with that we will learn to live happier, more productive lives.

When we learn to think at alpha and act at beta, we will be like the men in the Sufi story, for working in harmony can produce results that would be impossible otherwise.

Alpha is not only a state in which to relax; it is also a state of readiness - for improvement.

So ... R E L A X, It's Good For You.

Bibliography

Here are some books helped me understand and cope with tension, stress and distress, and the burnout I was experiencing at the end of my newspaper career back in 1975. These books deal with physical as well as psychological causes of stress and have helped me learn to lead a more relaxed, healthier life.

The Relaxation Response, Herbert Benson, William Morrow and Company, Inc., 1975

The Conquest of Frustration, Maxwell Maltz, Grosset & Dunlap, Inc., 1969

Type A Behavior and Your Heart, Meyer Friedman & Ray H. Rosenman, Alfred A. Knopf, 1974

Stress Without Distress, Hans Selye, J.B. Lippincott, 1974

Future Shock, A. Toffler, Random House, 1970

On the Psychology of Meditation, C. Naranjo and Robert Ornstein, Viking Press, 1971

Let's Eat Right to Keep Fit, Adelle Davis, Harcourt Brace Jovanovich, Inc., 1954

Sugar Blues, William Dufty, Chilton Book Company, 1975

Nutrition and Your Mind, George Watson, Harper & Row, 1972

Handbook to Higher Consciousness, Ken Keyes Jr., Living Love Publications, St. Mary, Kentucky, 1972

The Mystery of the Mind, Wilder Penfield, Princeton University Press, 1977

The Silva Mind Control Method, Jose Silva and Philip Miele, Simon & Schuster, 1977

How to be Your Own Best Friend, Mildred Newman and Bernard Berkowitz, Random House 1971

Acres of Diamonds, Russel H. Conwell, Fleming H. Revell Company, 1960

How to Win Friends and Influence People, Dale Carnegie, Simon and Schuster, 1936

The Greatest Salesman in the World, Og Mandino, Frederick Fell, 1968

Aerobics, Kenneth H. Cooper NLD., M. Evans and Company, 1968

You can readmore about what I have learned about dealing with stress and - more importantly - dealing with the things that cause stress in the books I have coauthored:

Jose Silva's Everyday ESP, Jose Silva Jr. with Ed Bernd Jr., New Page Books , 2007

The next three books are available in several eBook formats at www.Smashwords.com, and in Quality Paperback at Amazon.com.

Think and Grow Fit: Jose Silva's guide to Mental Training for Fitness and Sports, Jose Silva with Ed Bernd Jr.

Sales Power, the SilvaMind Method for Sales Professionals, Jose Silva with Ed Bernd Jr.

Jose Silva's UltraMind ESP System, by Ed Bernd Jr.

Ten most stressful jobs

In a study of 22,000 working men and women, the National Institute of Occupational Safety and Health came up with the ten "Best Stressed" jobs in the United States. The findings do not include specialized fields like air traffic controllers or fire fighters.

In order, the ten most stressful jobs are:

1 - Inspectors, those who do inspection tests in blue collar operations

2 - Health Technological Technicians

3 - Clinical Laboratory Technicians

4 - Miners and Mine Workers

5 - Industrial Laborers

6 - Warehouse Personnel

7 - Office Managers

8 - Public Relations Workers

9 - Licensed Practical Nurses

10- Waiters - not necessarily waitresses

The least stressful job is librarian. Also in low stress jobs are stock handlers, store checkout workers, college or university professors, office machine workers and bank tellers.

Scale of stressful situations

Loss of a spouse, by death or divorce, is the greatest stress faced by most men and women, according to two University of Washington Medical School psychiatrists.

Dr. Thomas H. Holmes and Dr. Richard H. Rahe, who devised a scale of stress for both good and bad experiences, discovered that ten times more widows and widowers die within the first year after the death of their spouses than all others in their age groups.

They also learned, from interviews with 394 individuals, that, compared to married persons, those who were divorced had twelve times the illness rate in the first year after their divorces.

Here is the Holmes-Rahe scale. The numbers denote the "impact" of each event in terms of stress, the highest impact being 100. The stress comes not from the actual event but from struggling to adjust to it.

Event - Impact

Death of Spouse - 100
Divorce - 73
Marital separation - 65
Jai I term - 63
Death of close family member - 63
Personal injury or illness - 53
Marriage - 50
Fired at work - 47
Marital reconciliation - 45
Retirement - 45
Change in health of family member - 44
Pregnancy - 40
Sex difficulties - 39
Gain of new family member - 39
Business readjustment - 39
Change in financial state - 38

Death of close friend - 37
Change to different line of work - 36
Change in number of arguments with spouse - 35
Mortgage over $10,000 - 31
Foreclosure of mortgage or loan - 30
Change in responsibilities at work - 29
Son or daughter leaving home - 29
Trouble with in-laws - 29
Outstanding personal achievement - 28
Wife begins or stops work - 26
Begin or end school - 26
Change in living conditions - 25
Revision of persona! habits - 24
Trouble with boss - 23
Change in work hours or conditions- 20
Change in residence - 20
Change in schools - 20
Change in recreation - 19
Change in church activities - 19
Change in social activities - 18
Mortgage or loan less than $10,000 - 17
Change in sleeping habits - 16
Change in number of family get-togethers - 15
Change in eating habits - 15
Vacation - 13
Christmas - 12
Minor law violations- 11

Resources

For information on genuine authentic Jose Silva courses and products that were authored by Jose Silva and have not been altered or changed by anone after his passing, contact:

Avlis Productions Inc.
P.O. Box 691809
Houston, TX 77269

1-866-322-8547 or 903-948-2312

www.SilvaCourses.com

To obtain books, recordings, home study courses, and free introductory lessons for the Silva UltraMind ESP System, please visit:

www.SilvaCourses.com

Genuine Jose Silva products to help you make the rest of your life the *best* of your life

Have you ever just thought of somebody and the phone rings and it's the same person? Or you say something at exactly the same time as a friend says it or thinks it! This is your own natural intuition. Now you can easily and quickly develop your ESP to help you make better decisions about health, relationships, business, personal growth.

Einstein claimed that he used only 10% of his mind, and the general public uses only about 3% or 4%. And that's what Jose Silva's revolutionary mind training systems are all about: learning to use more of your mind. There is no limit to how far you can go; there is no limit to what you can do, because there is no limit to the power of your mind.

Are you willing to be the very first "Neighborhood Healer" in your neighborhood? Yes, you can do this. And it only takes a few minutes to learn how. This is the wonderful gift that Jose Silva left us. All we are asking now is that you try it and see for yourself that you have the ability channel healing energy to help your loved ones.

Order these and other genuine Jose Silva products from:

www.SilvaCourses.com

Printed in Great Britain
by Amazon.co.uk, Ltd.,
Marston Gate.